WALKING AMONGST GIANTS

Trekking in the Annapurna Region

Nina Olsson

Grosvenor House
Publishing Limited

The right of Nina Olsson to be identified as the author of this
work has been asserted in accordance with Section 78
of the Copyright, Designs and Patents Act 1988

The book cover picture is copyright to Nina Olsson
The book cover artwork by David Bixter

This book is published by
Grosvenor House Publishing Ltd
Link House
140 The Broadway, Tolworth, Surrey, KT6 7HT.
www.grosvenorhousepublishing.co.uk

A CIP record for this book
is available from the British Library

ISBN 978-1-78623-244-1

This book is dedicated to all fellow travellers whose love for adventure will lead them everywhere. And to Joan, who followed me with her heart and imagination.

Giants of Nepal

Contents

PHOTOGRAPHIC PLATES

Back Cover: Jharkot area.

Front Cover: Annapurna 1.

Front full plate - various Mountains - Annapurnas, Dhaulagiri, Nilgiri, Machhaputchre and Everest.

Photographs 15 and 27 taken by Paul.
Photograph 50 taken by Nicky.
Photograph 77 taken by the Hotel Receptionist.
All other photographs taken by Nina.
All photographs printed by 'Photo Corner Ltd', Bebington, Wirral

Giants of Nepal

Preface

I decided that I wanted to visit Nepal. I suppose that it was an idea that had been simmering for at least three decades, so finally in my fifties, I felt it was time to go.

In the married phase of my life, my husband, two children Tim and Simon and I had been posted to Brunei, a wonderful three year posting with a Gurkha Rifles Regiment. We had met with the families around the camp, at the swimming pool and in the NAAFI shops. It was wonderful to glimpse into another culture.

I was at that time a volunteer presenter in the Brunei section of the British Forces Radio, where my programme immediately followed the Nepalese section. At the changeover, I was always met with a smiling face and we exchanged pleasantries as his music faded out, and mine played in. I was also once 'rescued' by a Gurkha soldier, holding a lit candle in a gale, after lightning had hit the transmitter aerial and blown out all of the electricity in the studio. (But that, as they say, is another story.)

An earlier connection had occurred, when in a Hampshire posting, the midwife at the birth of my youngest son was from Nepal, so I suppose it was inevitable that one day I would want to see their country myself.

All of that took place in the 1970s and life went on, with all of the general life events, raising children, school runs, following their hobbies and then suddenly there was just me.

Adventure time, and time to fulfil some of my dreams, and my first choice was Nepal.

The following account took place in 2002, when a very happy month was spent walking the trekking trails in Nepal. The information within being true to my knowledge at the time.

Sadly, in 2015 a huge earthquake devastated many areas of the country, affecting Kathmandu and other cities, towns and villages. Some of the buildings and areas listed may no longer exist. Durbar Square in Kathmandu suffered greatly, many of the ancient temples being destroyed. Fortunately, Pashupatinath escaped much of the devastation, Bodhnath, however, lost its tower.

Many historic buildings collapsed, and countless houses were flattened throughout the countryside, leaving over two million people homeless. A large rescue mission was mounted, and some of the infrastructure has since been reinstalled.

Some research was done using various sources including 'Wikipedia', other internet sites, guidebooks of Nepal, ACAP Leaflet, reminiscences, photographs and information from my journal.

My thanks to all involved: to Simon and Penny for their support, to Carl for fixing my computer just before I was about to throw it out of the window, to Christine for the main title, to the publishing house team for proofreading the manuscript, to Lez for help in designing the cover, to Paula for looking after my house and my cats, to Sandra for the party and my Mum and sisters Christine and Jean for their continuing support and interest. And to Paul and Nicky for their company on the trek, Bridget and Barry for their excellent organisational skills, and to our porters, Hum, Ashish, Amrit, Sante and Dorjee for all of their hard work.

To Tamsin, Becky and all staff at Grosvenor House Publishing Ltd. for their help, support, advice and encouragement.

Adventures in the Annapurna Conservation Area

"We paused in sheer astonishment. The sight of it banished every thought; we asked no questions, no comment, but simply looked …" borrowed from George Leigh Mallory

Introduction

A visit to Nepal, I decided, was just what I needed and wanted. Having travelled the world as an army wife, I again felt the stirrings of my 'adventure gene'.

I looked into the various areas, and decided reluctantly, that the Everest Base Camp trek was beyond my capabilities. I decided instead to go to the Annapurna Conservation Area. The more I learned about it, the more certain I was that I had made the right choice.

Preparation

The initial detailed plans took about eight months. As with any plans of that nature, I had been saving money in my 'adventure' account for over a year, to ensure that I had adequate funding. I obtained special permission from work and was given my leave all in one session.

I looked at various companies and decided to go with 'Nepalese Trails', run by a husband and wife team, Bridget and Barry. I paid my deposit and received an information pack, which included a kit list.

I was never an outdoors adventure kind of person, so buying clothing and equipment of that type was a whole new experience. I proceeded to tick things off the list as I went along. I also started leaving the car at home and walking everywhere I could, increasing the distances each time.

My boots were my first acquisition, I knew as soon as I put them on, they were the ones for me. I had tried on many pairs, but only this pair was right immediately. There was to be a great deal of walking over various types of terrain, so good fitting, comfortable boots were essential.

I also bought a good sleeping bag, a large rucksack with a back protector, thermal underwear, socks, whistle, compass and other items such as a compact first aid kit. Most importantly, I bought a book telling me about the region, the people and the customs.

Nearer the leaving date other items were purchased, such as glucose tablets, energy tablets, iodine water treatment tablets, wet wipes, prickly heat ointment. It was important to ensure that I carried a good supply of plasters, painkillers, diarrhoea tablets, replacement electrolyte packs and all of the prescription drugs that I would require over the time period. I had the necessary inoculations done (listed in the appendix).

I bought a journal in which to store my thoughts during the trip.

A friend of a friend had heard about the trip and asked about joining in. This was Nicky. Absolutely yes, it meant someone to share the rooms with, to share the adventure, and the conversations that followed.

Speaking of conversations, Joan, the mother of my daughter-in-law, Penny, was an avid armchair traveller and was most interested in my trip. Originally from Burma, but she had lived in India for some years. She had wanted to make the trip to the shrine at Muktinath but was never able to.

One evening, I packed my rucksack with my kit and took it to her house. We had a great evening, unpacking everything and discussing what I was taking, equipment, clothes etc., all the whys and wherefores. Before I left she gave me some pencils and notepads to take for the schools, and also two small round tins containing fruit cake. The cake had its own story to tell later on.

By July it was time to apply for the Nepalese visa from the London Embassy.

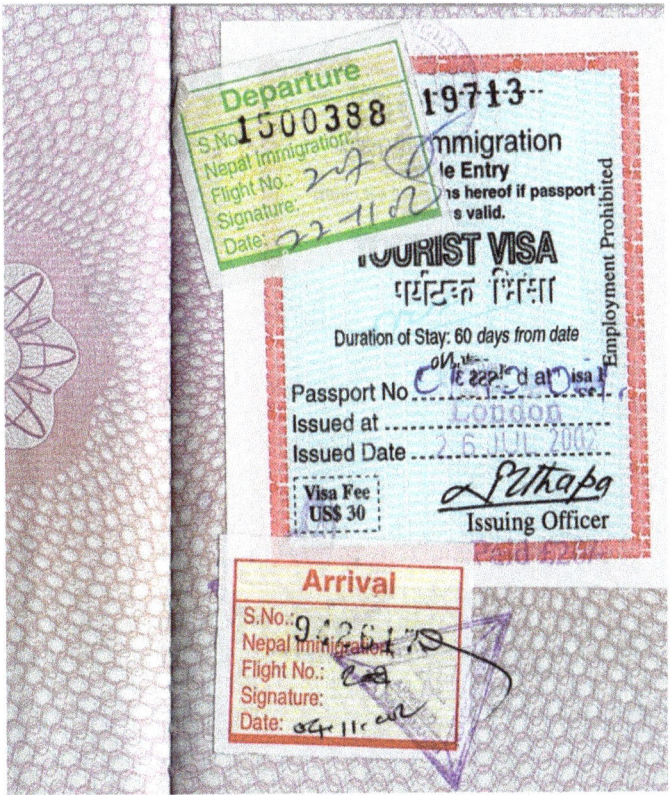

October came, and I bought the films for the camera (pre-digital times for me). I was taking my pride and joy, my Olympus SLR.

Packing had always been a problem for me, what to take clothes-wise, and what, along with the essentials, could be fitted into the smallest spaces. I needed to keep in mind that the porters would have to carry the large rucksack, while I would carry other smaller items in the daypack. And, there was, of course, the tiny problem of getting it all to Nepal in the first place.

As usual, I left home with far too much, resembling a pack mule that I later saw out on the trail.

Setting off

Nicky and I were due to catch a coach to London on November 1st. We had decided to go a day early as there was an exhibition on in London, called 'Body Works' that we wanted to see, and fascinating it was too. But wait, I get ahead of myself. Rewind to the night before.

"It was a dark and stormy night...", well actually it was a bit damp and the moon shone brightly (salute to Neil Gaiman and Terry Pratchett), but it was Halloween. As we were due to leave the next morning, our friends had put on a sort of bon-voyage with a gothic twist. We wore our finest costumes and partied into the night.

Next morning, rucksacks at the ready, it was time to go, the last night's frivolities almost forgotten, being supplanted by the excitement of the day.

We had an overnight stay at the airport hotel, then time to book in for our flight (I had a little twitch as my films went through the X-ray machine, I would be devastated if they all turned out to be blank on my return home). And so, to meet the third member of our party. A very pleasant guy name of Paul, from the Midlands.

We flew Gulf Air, excellent flight, comfortable, good food and we were touching down in Abu Dhabi in what seemed like no time at all. We had a four-hour layover before the next stage of the journey, so over coffee and tea, we got to know each other.

The airport building was amazing, decorated in part with green and blue mosaics, and shops that we could not afford to look in, never mind buy anything.

Originally there had been other people booked on the trip, but they had pulled out because of the unrest in the country. We, too, were given that option but had decided to still go, and the company was fine with that. And an excellent decision it was too.

Arrival

We finally arrived at Tribhuvan airport in Kathmandu. Once through customs we were met by Bridget and Barry who had decided to join the party, making our eventual numbers, with our porters, up to ten.

It was all incredibly exciting.

About Nepal

A small country, barely 600 miles in length and 100 miles across. The Himalayan mountain range runs from Pakistan in the west, to Bhutan in the east. India forms the southern border, and Chinese Tibet the northern border.

The population is made up of groups of mixed origins; tribal groups such as Newari, Rai, Gurung, Limbu, Magar and Sherpa, some Tibetan peoples and some from Indian backgrounds. The national language is Nepalese, but many different dialects are spoken in the towns and villages.

The two main religions are Hinduism and Buddhism, although there are other religions practised throughout the country.

Nepal was previously a multi-party democracy with the King at its head but, following the civil war, in 2008 it became a republic with a multi-party system.

The Annapurna Conservation Area Project (ACAP)

The project was set up in 1986 and was designed to integrate community development and conservation of the environment and habitats of the various peoples and animals living in the area.

Entry permits are mandatory. Entry fees are also required, the funds from which are put back into the communities for schools, development of infrastructure and the conservation of cultural heritage.

The idea was to encourage people to share in the responsibilities of their environment, to build up and protect their areas and everything within them, plant, animal or human. Thus far, this has been a very successful venture.

Minimum Impact Code

Visitors to the area are asked to adhere to the Code.
Respect the Environment.
Do not light wood fires.
Use the Lodges.
Hunting is prohibited.
Fishing permits are required.
Do not leave behind litter or plastic bottles.
Do not soil water sources and bury your waste.
Do not disturb wildlife.
Do not remove animals or plants.
Respect local customs, privacy, your own and the local population.

Trekkers are advised to never travel alone, hire a guide if necessary. Take warm clothing. Purify your own water. Carry a good Medical Kit and any pills that are required, prescription and painkillers.

Learn about the signs and symptoms of Altitude Sickness and what to do. Take rests and drink plenty.

Facts and Figures:

Size – 7,629 km squared.

Altitude – between 790m (Khudi) to 8091m at Annapurna I.

Wildlife species – numerous plants, over 100 different mammals, almost 500 species of birds, also reptiles and amphibians.

Facilities – there are project offices throughout the region, information centres, museums, check posts, health clinics and hospitals, airports of varying sizes and large numbers of lodges on the various trek routes.

Tourism forms the largest part of the economy of the region.

(Information taken from 'The Annapurna Ways' leaflet published by the King Mahendra Trust for Nature Conservation now known as The National Trust for Nature Conservation (NTNC).

Himalayan Song

We came, we saw,

We gasped at the absolute majesty of it all,

As we learnt their names,

Each mountain presented itself to us,

Magical names like Machhapuchhre,

Nilgiri, Dhaulagiri, the Annapurnas,

Lajong and Sagarmatha,

A quick glimpse of an image that will stay forever,

Smiling patient people, hard pressed but hopeful,

In forests of green, too numerous to count.

Sung to us in Nepali by our guide companions. November 2002

Chapter One

Kathmandu

Kathmandu is the largest metropolis in the Himalayan Hill Region, and the capital city of Nepal. During medieval times the city was known as Kantipur, *kanti* meaning beauty (light) and *pur* meaning place.

The plane touched down gently and the door opened to a completely new world. The first thing I noticed after the surge of heat that met me, was the beautiful smell of burning wood, the fragrance filled the air, the smell of which still evokes amazing memories to this day.

Once through customs and luggage retrieval, we were met by Bridget and Barry, who presented us with floral necklaces made from Marigolds. A lovely friendly, traditional greeting. We were taken to our hotel through the narrow streets of the city's Thamel district.

So much to see already, it was the Festival of Lights. The houses were lit with decorations, bunting and candles everywhere; traditionally to attract wealth and wellbeing for the next year – rather like the Lion and Dragon dances that took place worldwide at Chinese New Year. This was the New Year celebrations of the Newari people, for their year 1123.

The airport had been so calm, but once out into the streets the clamour was incredible, there was noise, horns blaring, people talking loudly, instant chaos. Everywhere, everything and everyone, so striking, a million rainbows in front of our eyes. A joy of just being, contrasted by the silent sacred cows that wandered the streets.

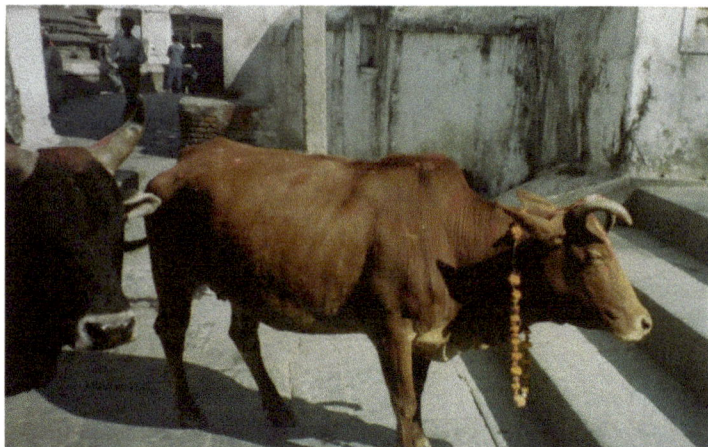

We arrived at our hotel, The Kantipur Temple House, down at the end of a narrow street. An old-style building, but with modern facilities. A friendly doorman welcomed us with the Nepalese greeting of "Namaste".

Nicky and I settled into our room. Before our evening meal, we spent time on the roof terrace, where a beautiful butterfly settled on Paul's hand. We took it as an omen that we were welcome in this most fascinating country.

Darkness had fallen as we walked back from the restaurant. Bridget and Barry had for many years, lived in Nepal and spoke the language fluently, so they were able to give us insight into the noisy, fascinating city.

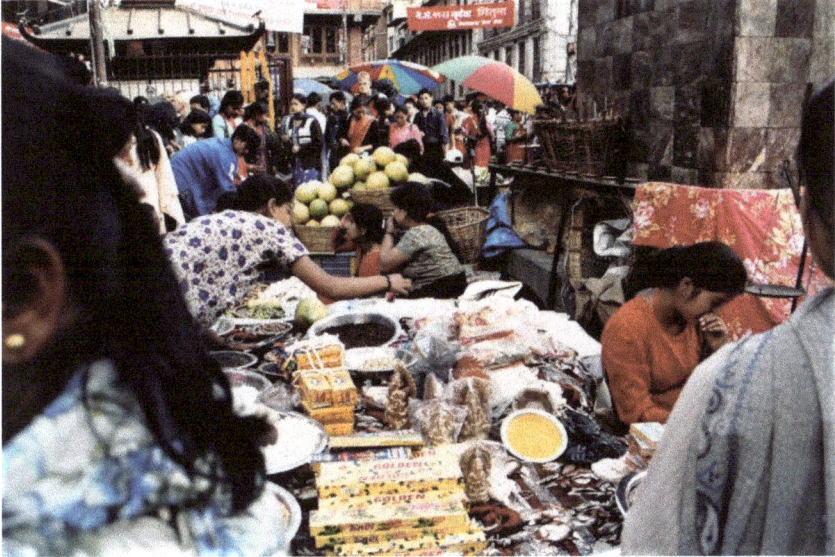

The roads were teeming with all manner of vehicles, cars, buses, motorbikes, taxis – many run on diesel and kerosene, most of which I doubted would have been legal on English roads, but here they were very much part of the embroidery of the city.

Back at the hotel, discussions took place regarding the itinerary for the next few weeks, after which it was definitely time for bed.

We arose early, into the coolness of the morning. A very good breakfast was enjoyed by all, then time to visit the Pashupatinath Temple. This was a large Hindu complex. The temple is dedicated to Lord Shiva and stretches both sides of the Bagmati river. Nepal is multi-denominational with Hinduism and Buddhism being the main religions.

Shrines to other deities surround the main temple, such as those to Ganesh, the elephant-headed son of Shiva and Parvati.

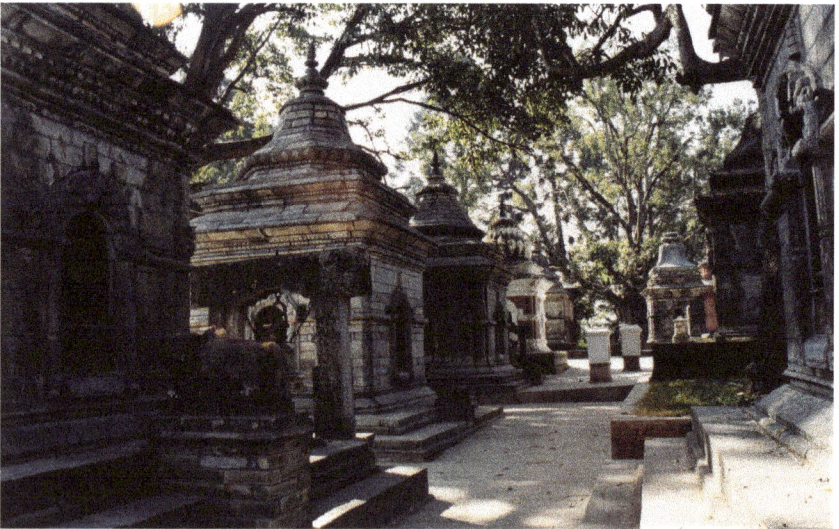

A statue of Shiva's vehicle, Nandi the Bull, lies inside the main building.

The temple, besides being a centre for worship and pilgrimage, was also a place for the cremations of the bodies of the dead. A solemn, respectful ceremony carried out by the relatives of the deceased. A great contrast to the throngs of other people there who came to pray or just to 'stand and stare'. Occasionally Gurkha soldiers would wander by, and we heard the 'Last Post' being played at one of the cremations.

Gurkha soldiers were originally chosen from the Gorkha region and had been part of the British Army since the early nineteenth century. They have seen action in many areas and are known for their bravery and loyalty, having won 12 Victoria Cross medals in their history.

The full circle of life was on show, from babes in their mother's arms, through many different generations, to the very old.

We left and walked through a wooded area on our way to the next site, the Buddhist Temple Bodhnath. There were family groups of monkeys playing in the woods, in my enthusiasm to photograph them I got too close. The next minutes saw me fleeing down the hill chased by two adult monkeys. A little scary but they were, after all, defending their families and their territory.

Everything in this country was to be a steep learning curve, in every sense of the words.

On to the Bodhnath Temple, one of the largest centres of Tibetan Buddhism in the world. A truly magnificent sight, with its 'all-seeing eyes' (harmika) and saffron stained walls. Throughout the day, the dye was thrown at the walls in an arc, to represent Lotus petals. We were able to go up on to the building where it was the custom to walk clockwise around the outer levels. There were a number of Buddhist Monks following the practice, as did we.

There were many monks at the site, some as young as five years old.

A number of prayer wheels were located around the area.

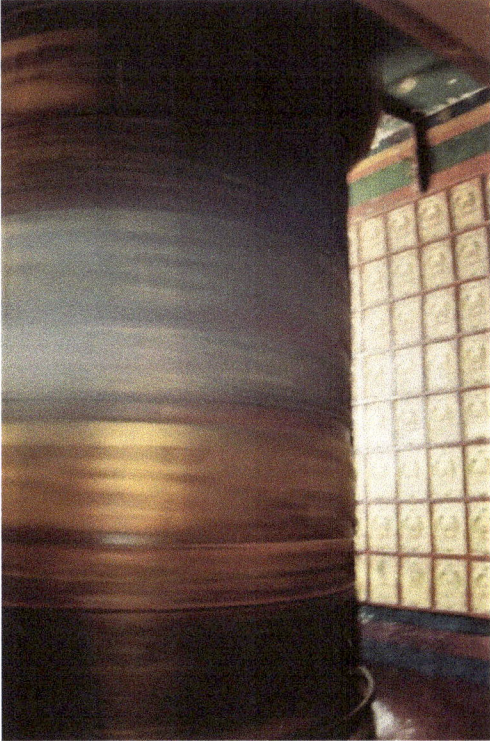

Many small shops were present on the site and a large number of street vendors selling all manner of goods. I was told to say 'pahile nai eka cha' or something that sounded like that, which meant "I have already got one". One seller tried to outwit me saying that it meant "I want to buy" – it did not work.

I enjoyed the visits to the temples and was struck by the people who, though poor by our standards, had a look of contentment about them. Sadly, this was not the case for the whole of Nepal, particularly in the countryside, where Maoist uprisings had taken hold.

Our next stop was Durbar Square, with its many temples, market stalls and hosts of people milling around – locals, visitors and us.

Radiant colours everywhere, in the clothes, the goods on display and the banners and flags. We saw Swamis surveying the scene with their distinctive face paint.

It was market day and around each stall, lively, loud bartering could be heard. Added to which there were the vehicles, mainly motorbikes, with whole families perched on them. Quite a balancing act, I had enough trouble just keeping my own balance in my biking days.

We climbed to the top of a temple overlooking the square, from where we surveyed and photographed the scene, a UNESCO world heritage site whose palaces once housed the Malla and Shah kings, previous rulers of the city. From one building we saw the figures of Shiva and Parvati looking out, as they kept watch over the square.

I think that I was still a little 'journey-lagged' as I found that I tired very quickly, so I was glad of the rest, perched on high.

Our last temple visit was to the Kumari Bahal, the residence of the living goddess.

The Kumari was chosen from a selection of girls between four and five years old. She had to fulfil a number of criteria, some physical and some spiritual, then once chosen she would live in the Bahal as the incarnation of the living goddess, coming out only to take part in the Indra Jatra Festival. She remained in the home until puberty or suffered blood loss from any source, such as a wound, at which time a new girl was chosen.

Following a rest back at the hotel, it was time to go out for our evening meal in the Thamel district. What a place, teeming with people in their bright attire. So many vehicles, noisy, horns honking, belching out exhaust fumes, I do not think I saw anything newer than 20 years old. However, they were still serviceable. There were bazaars selling many items including the normal tourist memorabilia. There were roadside eating houses with open frontages, where the smells of the different foods on offer came wafting on to the streets. There were old dogs who followed until you fed them and then went off to find the next benefactor.

A local pickpocket half-heartedly tried to steal from us and was astounded when Barry told him to "go away" in his own language. His face was a picture. There were many beggars on the streets, often small children, whose parents lurked nearby. It was very hard to say no and ignore them, but it was not recommended to give them money, but instead to donate to the local schools and shelters.

It was New Year for the Newari people and in the Thamel district the streets and houses were decorated, rather like western houses at Christmas. Even late into the evening, families were out on the streets, musicians playing, music coming from houses and restaurants, and buildings festooned with lights. All this and the air heavy with the smell of scented wood fires. I was mesmerized.

11

The next day we had booked a flight to see Mount Everest. We arrived at the airport around 7am to await our flight with Buddha Airways. A small airport, with small planes which serviced the internal and tourist routes. We presented our tickets and were ready to board. The plane was tiny, only eighteen seats overall, seven down each side and four across the back. We were a party of five, the rest being other tourists. Two pilots and an air hostess completed the line-up.

We took off, and the plane was soon at its cruising height of 7620 metres (25,000 feet). We flew alongside the Himalayan range. What a view, the mountains ranged in height from the 7,000+ metre giants to the 8,000+ metre mammoths. We saw the whole range stretching out from Kathmandu to Everest.

We each had a map with every mountain named. Magical names like Cho Oyu, Gyachung Kang, Pumori, Nuptse, and Lhotse. Each with a peak more striking than the last, until in the distance we could see one peak standing proud over the others. We were each given the opportunity to go to the cockpit to take photographs.

The sight of Everest, Nepalese name Sagarmatha, or Chomolungma in the Tibetan tongue, was truly superb, with its glistening white peak which rose up to meet the blue sky. The highest place on the entire planet. The photographs taken through the plane windows in no way reflected the true stature and total magnificence of what was in front of our eyes. It was no wonder that people had been so drawn to it over the centuries.

My opening saying was a quote from George Mallory (1922 and 1924 Everest Expeditions) and was in fact in reference to Everest, but I thought that it equally suited the Annapurna mountains and region.

13

Lunchtime saw us back at our hotel. A trip to Bungamati had been arranged for the afternoon. This was a small town, little changed for centuries, and famous as the winter home of the Rato Machindra god of Patan. Largely untouched by modern living, the overriding feeling, to me anyway, was that of poverty, and yet there were many smiling faces. Women were using the courtyard of the temple, to dry out the freshly sieved corn, brought in from the nearby fields. The men were in a nearby hall, drinking beer and playing cards – the way of life here, I guess.

One enterprising family had collected various artefacts and opened their home as a small museum so, after a fee had been negotiated, we went to visit. They were as fascinated with Nicky's hair (strawberry blonde), as we were with their exhibits.

The jeep bounced back along the pitted roads to Kathmandu. A rest, then food. We went to a very bohemian style restaurant, Kilroys, complete with indoor waterfall. The food was good and plentiful, besides the dahl bhat, chicken, rice, black lentils and curd and chilli dips, we had bread and butter pudding, a favourite we later found in many of the lodges. I ate the lot, I told myself that it was needed to build up my reserves for the trek, nothing at all to do with just being plain piggy.

A last walk through the city back to the hotel, and time to write up our diaries, then bed. Words weren't always enough to convey the feelings, sights, sounds, smells, colours, breath-taking beauty and the joy of the people and the country, but I have done my best.

Certainly, a city of contrasts.

Barry had earlier sorted out our entry permits for the Annapurna region, which were a requirement for entry into the Conservation Area. Tomorrow would be the start of the adventure, starting with a road trip to Pokhara.

Note :

1. This Entry Permit is valid for single entry only. The permit holder can enter the designated places within the Conservation Area.

2. Person entering Conservation Area shall abide by the National Park and Wildlife Conservation Act 2029 B.S. (1973) and the Regulations made under this Act.

3. This Entry Permit must be carried during the entire trip and should be shown if the concerned personnel of the Conservation Area want to check it.

MAILING ADDRESS

P.O. Box : 3712, Kathmandu, Nepal
Phone : (977-1) 526571 and 526 573
Fax : (977-1) 526 570

King Mahendra Trust for Nature Conservation

TRUST FOR NATURE

KING MAHENDRA

CONSERVATION

NEPAL. 1982

ANNAPURNA CONSERVATION AREA

NON REFUNDABLE

ENTRY PERMIT

Chapter Two

Pokhara

It was time to move on. We were up at 5.15 am, breakfasted and packed ready to embark on our next phase of the trip, courtesy of a long wheelbase jeep. We took just what we thought we would need and left some of the luggage at the hotel to pick up at the end of the trip. Lessening the load for our porters.

The roads around the city and immediate outlying areas were pretty good.

However, once further out into the Kathmandu Valley, it became obvious as to why the jeep was so necessary. We had a good driver, so felt safe, however the constant blowing of the vehicle horns, though annoying at first, after a while was less so – I tried to make a tune of it.

It reminded me of another time, in my student days, in the then Yugoslavia, when a fellow hitch-hiker and I were travelling between Split and Dubrovnik. The coastal road had flooded, so all traffic was diverted up into the hills. The roads were very narrow, at some points little more than tracks, and became gridlocked, with movement only at certain passing points.

Naturally, people became very frustrated, including our fiery Italian driver who joined in with the horn blowing. As the vehicles were of many different makes, the horn sounds were different. Before too long there was a full orchestral piece being played.

Back to Nepal, once we had cleared the heavy traffic we were able to enjoy the scenery which was, of course, a pure delight. As it was still very early there was mist on the hills, but the view back down the valley was spectacular. We crossed several rivers and stopped to photograph the white-water junction of the Trishuli and Seti rivers.

As we drove on, hills would appear in and out of the mist. We saw terraces where crops including rice, were being grown. We passed red mud house (Rato mato), some with brightly painted trucks sitting outside, sometimes buses with motifs such as "love every child and tree equally", vehicles for work situations, motorbikes, but very few individually owned cars.

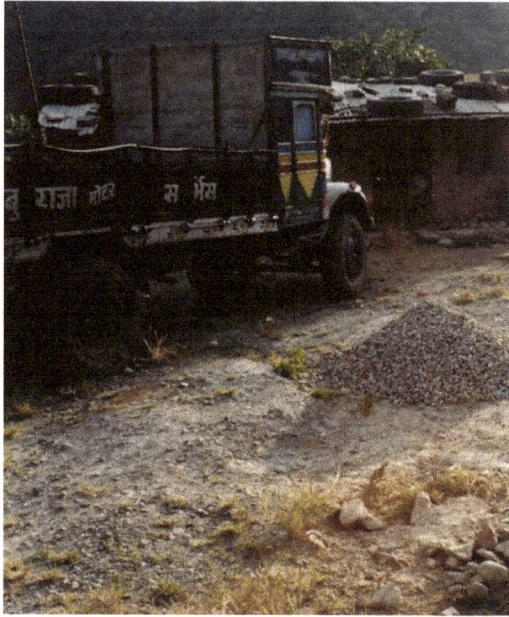

We stopped at a tea house. What a beautiful place, neat gardens with tropical flowers in abundance, wafting their perfumes on to the gentle breeze. The temperature had risen, time for the sunscreens and hats.

Our next stop was Pokhara.

What a busy place, shops galore – food shops, material and sewing shops, trinket shops and even shops where you could hire porters for your treks, and mountain porters for the more adventurous. There were a great number of Europeans in colourful 'hippy type' clothing, it was like stepping back to the late 1960s, early 70s.

Our hotel was cool and welcoming. After a quick rest, we went down to the lake. This was Phewa Lake.

What a stunning scene greeted us. The area was surrounded by mountains reflected in the mostly tranquil water. A few houses hugged the lakeside, while small fishing boats, canoes and rowing boats bobbed gently on the lake edge. The mountains with their snow-laden peaks glistened in the sunlight, and the magnificent Machhapuchhre (known as the Fish Tail mountain), stood proudly over the whole setting. I do not have enough words to describe the breath-taking majesty of the whole scene.

We hired a rowing boat, and as the sun started to set, Barry and I went out to the middle of the lake. We saw monkeys, kingfishers, all manner of other birds, and brightly dressed people going about their business. Naturally, photographs were taken, then we just sat. I felt very insignificant among all of that splendour but privileged to be seeing it.

As the sun set lower in the sky, the colours reflected in the snow caps, started to change. Firstly, a subtle pink gradually deepening to a golden orange. A sight that deeply embedded itself in my psyche.

On returning to the shoreline I went to a Tibetan stall selling jewellery and knick-knacks. I bought a beautiful bangle with turquoise stones and an engraved Buddhist text. I wore it for the rest of the trip.

I met up with the others as we walked back to the hotel. A welcome meal and bed for the night.

The next day we were to go to the Tibetan Monastery at Tashiling, a village an hour's walk through the fields. On the way there we passed a hydroelectric dam.

Many families were there, who made use of the clear waters, washing their clothes and their children, all of which were left to dry on the warm sun-bathed rocks. There were also a number of young men from the local police academy doing their laundry.

A young Nepali man caught up with us, who turned out to be our head porter, Hum, a gentle man who we instantly liked. We sat drinking our boiled water, the taste of which I definitely needed to get used to, even with the orange flavoured tablets. After the introductions, we walked on, through fields where a group of women were cutting the corn.

Very hard work in the blistering sun but accompanied by singing and waving to us. We were invited to work with them. We graciously declined, I do not think I would have lasted half an hour. It was very hot, the temperatures soon soared after the cool morning starts, and breathing was a bit of a problem, never mind toiling in the fields.

At the end of our walk was a small monastery where we were proudly shown around by a monk of about 9 years old. It had a Buddhist Temple at its heart, with mandalas, bright multicoloured banners and a portrait of the Dalai Lama, the High Priest of Tibetan Buddhism. Two large solar dishes set up in the courtyard provided the power for the whole complex.

On the return route, we visited the Devi Falls, a place where the river plunges down through a hole in the ground, making a large, incredibly deep, mostly unseen waterfall. The area was surrounded by Tibetan craft shops. We were asked where we were from. I told them England, and how cold it was there at this time of year. An elderly lady nearby said sadly, "We like it cold." I thought of how they must have felt, being dispossessed of their homeland on the high Tibetan Plateau and sent to hot countries like India and Nepal.

Later, we went for our evening meal, chicken with a salad and raw vegetables cut into beautiful butterfly and flower shapes. A great pity, because we had been told not to eat raw foods as they would have been washed in the local water. We felt awful sending it back uneaten.

I had a little cotton jacket made at one of the sewing shops, long sleeved, ideal for wear in the temples. I was impressed at the speed at which it was made and was pleased with the result.

The next day our trek was due to start in earnest, our entry permits had been obtained in Kathmandu. There were a number of customs posts on our route where all paperwork, passports and the like, would need to be presented and checked.

Chapter Three

Jomsom

Up at 5am, it was getting earlier. Our jeep took us to the airport for the flight up to Jomsom. There was a very good reason for the early start. The plane needed to have landed at Jomsom and also made the return journey to Pokhara by 10am.

The route between the mountains became a wind tunnel later in the day and flying was an impossibility for the small planes. (Larger planes were not feasible, as we soon saw, on espying the landing strip.)

Once in the air, the views were absolutely spectacular. We flew over the Kathmandu Valley where we could see many villages each surrounded by areas of cultivated land, a patchwork of fields and terraces.

We sat admiring the view and chatted excitedly about the adventures to come. The plane veered to the right, and we could see ahead a narrow passage between the mountains.

We flew into the space between two mountains, Dhaulagiri and Nilgiri, which stood like monumental sentinels guarding the pass. The wind had started to blow just enough to rock the plane, a bit scary but exhilarating for all that. We were not at a great height and I wondered idly about what would happen if we went down. I came to the conclusion that if it was my time, apart from regrets for my family, then what a spectacular place for it to happen.

Of course, my fears were totally unfounded, the flight took place every day, just routine for all involved.

It was quite amazing seeing the mountains so close up.

I found that in my whole time in Nepal, the views became more and more outstanding everywhere you looked. I took many, many photographs.

The plane banked, and we made ready for the landing. The runway was short, oh my, very short, but the pilots were well used to it. The landing was relatively smooth, and we came to rest in front of a blue-roofed airport terminal building. I had enjoyed the flight, but if I am honest, I was a bit relieved to get off. We watched the plane take off again for the return journey. It must have been all of 8am.

Here we met the rest of the porters. They were at the airport, having spent several days walking up from Kathmandu. They presented each of us with a welcome prayer type scarf, a lovely gesture which made us feel very special. So, this was our first meeting with Ashish, Amrit, Sante and Dorjee. The other member, Hum, had flown up, with us. Our party was now complete.

Jomsom, as we had been told, was a very different landscape. A little how I imagined the American 'Wild West' would have been in the 1880s, minus the guns but with the townsfolk, hotels and horses.

We passed a procession of porters, carrying very heavy loads (dokos), followed by two, I presume, climbers carrying – nothing.

We were shocked. They were far too heavily laden, even our lads could be heard muttering in disapproval.

We booked into our hotel, breakfasted, then following a short rest we went to see the local cultural museum. An important visit as the whole region was designated a conservation area. Firstly, we were shown a video on how the concept was being implemented and then given a talk on acceptable behaviour within the area. The whole scheme worked very closely with the local people, conserving the land and its wildlife, and had brought with it a small degree of prosperity.

We saw costumes, artefacts and photographs of the various peoples of the region. There was also a very large wall map showing the cities, towns and villages of Nepal. The lads showed us where their homes were situated. Amrit, from near the Indian border, Ashish from southern Nepal, Sante was from the Gorkha region, Dorjee was a Sherpa from the Everest area and Hum was from western Nepal.

Back at the hotel, I began to feel a little queasy, due I think to the change in altitude. As yet I was not acclimatised, but that situation would change as Bridget and Barry had been careful in their planning of the route, giving us enough rest time at each height to allow our bodies to adjust.

Our hotel was called the Mona Lisa, complete with a mural on the wall. I had seen the real painting in the Louvre in Paris and was surprised at how small it was, especially in comparison with other paintings there. However, the magic of it soon drew you in, and you could not help but smile back, it was hard to tear yourself away from her gaze. A little like what was happening here in Nepal, with its magnificent vistas and smiling people.

In the afternoon, I decided to stay at the hotel to rest and recharge my batteries. Ashish stayed too, down in the lounge, just in case I needed anything. Such caring already. I hoped that the nausea would soon pass, particularly as this was a relatively low altitude, and I had come to experience the country not to lie in bed.

Of course, I woke up feeling much better and was able to join Ashish for a version of afternoon tea, and it gave me chance to chat with him. I enjoyed meeting all of our travelling companions, very giggly we found out later, with a lovely innocent type of humour. Even on this short acquaintance I found them all to be very attentive, not the least intrusive, but with our welfare at heart.

I went for the evening meal, and opted for tomato soup, a family remedy for all ills. Always worked wonders. Afterwards, a team briefing on the adventures to come, the what, where and when; and of course, the safety factors to be built in.

Off to bed, even though it was only 8.15pm, but we needed to be prepared for a very early start. A pattern for the rest of our trek.

Chapter Four

On the trail to Kagbeni

Another early rise, although we did manage a slight sleep in, it was 5.45am. We had a good breakfast and made ready for the walking phase of the trip.

We were to carry our daypacks (small rucksacks) with our cameras, drinks, medicines, sun cream and so on, while our assigned porter –mine was Amrit – carried our large packs. We each made space for the porters to stow their belongings in the lid section of the rucksacks.I had tried to make mine as light as I could. My goodness, it was almost as big as he was, I don't know how he managed over such terrain. He was not even out of breath!

We walked for a couple of hours, following the Kali Gandaki River, which at that time of year was only present in small streams, but still with some force in the flow. I really struggled up one of the hills, I really should have made more effort to up my fitness levels before I came. I am not of a sporty nature and the concept of anything gym related filled me with horror. Big mistake.

We stopped at the Eklebatti Tea House for a very welcome break. Here we were introduced to chiya, the Nepalese version of tea. It was a sweet spiced drink that we soon got used to drinking. There were a number of people at the place, mostly trekkers, some locals and a Tibetan lady who spent the whole time surveying the scene and twisting her meditation beads.

After our break, we continued on through the gorge towards Kagbeni.

We passed other walkers and stood aside while a laden horse train came by, carrying foodstuffs for the outlying villages.

All animal trains had right of way, the lead animals wearing large cowbells to warn of their coming. It was very important on the cliff paths to ensure you were not caught on the 'drop' side of the track as stepping backwards could prove fatal.

The scenery was interesting, with arid looking areas set against snow-topped mountains. The landscape looked as if it could have been on the surface of the moon, apart from the few bridges crossing the gorge.

In the distance Nilgiri stood, its commanding presence dominating the scene unfolding before us. It was not just the thinner air that affected our breathing.

We walked for another two hours and passed a number of mani stones, (Tibetan prayers inscribed in stone in high altitude places). Finally, we saw Kagbeni, our overnight stop, in the distance. The next day we were to start our first uphill section, a climb of 610 metres, approximately 2000 feet, so a great change in altitude.

Kagbeni, in keeping with many towns and villages, had an impressive entrance gate, the ceiling of which was decorated with Buddhist Mandalas.

We found our lodge, pre-booked by Sante, who had gone on ahead to make sure everything was in readiness for the arrival of the rest of the party. This happened at every stop-over. We rested for a short while. This lodge was bigger than most, with fair sized rooms and thankfully a comfortable bed.

Later, we sat out on the terrace, drinking tea and surveying our surroundings. Stacked in every corner was wood being stored for cooking and heating, especially for the winter to come. Only fallen wood was allowed to be collected, it was not permitted to chop down trees in the conservation area.

Refreshed, we went for a walk around the town. An interesting place with a mixture of stone houses, small hotels, and a shop which to our surprise sold European beers and chocolate bars. The town was bustling with people going about their business, other trekkers wandering about, and yaks grazing on the small patches of greenery. On a hill overlooking the town was a Buddhist Monastery, with a row of prayer wheels leading up to the entrance. Tradition dictated that you spun them as you passed.

There was also a large fort on the outskirts, this was the border with Upper Mustang, a restricted area leading through what was Tibet into China itself. A special, very expensive visa was needed to pass through the Mustang valley. There was a police post at the border to ensure there were no illegal crossings. The only people with free access were those from Mustang, who came through Kagbeni for trading purposes.

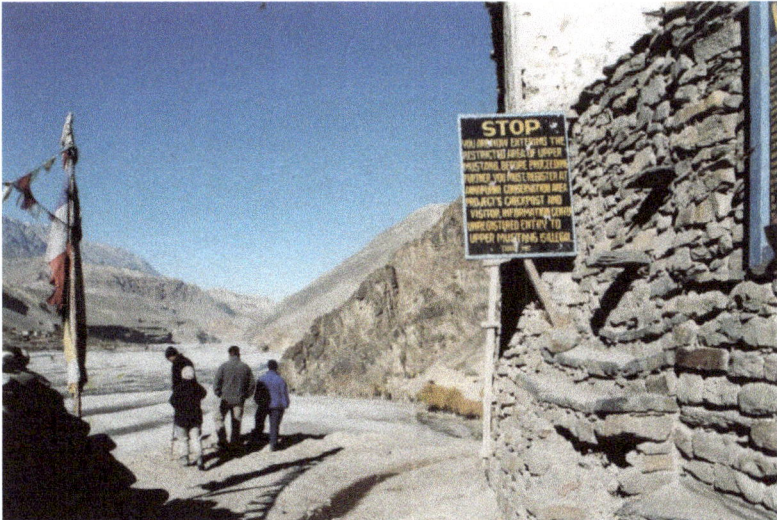

We returned to our hotel and after our evening meal, Nicky, Paul and I went up to the roof terrace to stargaze. I have never seen so many, so clear and so close, it was like having a star quilt wrapped around you, a truly magnificent sight.

I woke early and looked out of the window at the track we were due to climb up to Jharkot, then on to Muktinath.

Oh, my word, it looked very steep.

Chapter Five

Jharkot and Muktinath

I was right, it was very steep. My breathing was already laboured. Of course, I knew that the trek was going to be uphill for much of it and I had tried to improve my fitness levels before I left home. I mused briefly on what would have happened if I had opted for the Everest base camp option – 'casi-vacked' out I imagine. And this was just the foothills of the mountains, nowhere near a snowy peak.

I thought about the mountaineers, especially the ones from the earlier decades, 1920s – Mallory et al, 1950s – Edmund Hillary's party and 1970s – people like Chris Bonington. I had a sneaking respect for them, even though I thought they were all mad.

Some of the mountains in front of us were the 8000 metre-plus giants – staggering. I was content to just photograph them. I stopped on many occasions to capture the view, well that and to get my breath back.

The early morning air was very cold and prickled your nose as you breathed, and because of the thinner atmosphere, deeper breaths had to be taken. To say that the scenery and experience was breath-taking was literally true.

We stopped at a plateau and looked back over the scene. Deep valleys, orchards, small villages, chequerboard fields with next year's crops, all surrounded by the magnificent mountains.

I had mistakenly thought that the mountains would appear as if in a line, but of course, they were all around, we were forever 'stepping on the toes of giants'.

We rested, had some water and energy bars before moving on. I cannot tell you how 'jaw-droppingly' amazing the whole experience was; just when you thought that you had seen something that could not be bettered, around the corner was something more spectacular.

Eventually, we could see the roofs of the houses at Jharkot, a large village and our next stop.

We were to be there for a couple of nights, as part of the acclimatisation process. Once there, we were told we had walked up 2,500 feet, no wonder we were all so tired. (I was going to use a more explicit word, but for the sake of decency, I have gone with tired.)

After a rest and late lunch, we went for a walk around the town.

A cluster of houses clung on to the banks of the hills, with narrow dirt roads criss-crossing the area. There was a large field in the centre ready for planting. A stone fort sat overlooking the town, no longer in use, but I had no doubt that the townspeople would have ably defended themselves if called upon to do so. A red painted monastery held the most commanding position.

A young boy of about ten years old tagged along with us and became our guide. He had little English, but we were surprised and impressed that he knew any of our language in such a remote place. Hand gestures sufficed perfectly well anyway. He took us up to the monastery whose walls were decorated with scenes from Buddhist stories, and also a large depiction of the 'Wheel of Life'.

As night fell, people returned from their labours in the fields, women chattering loudly, followed by the men herding the animals, cows and yaks, before disappearing into the houses as the sun went down.

There was so much activity, then suddenly it was all quiet in the darkness. We were told that the reason for this was to keep the animals safe from the night-time predators that came down from higher ground looking for prey.

No night time walkabouts for us then.

Following our meal, it was fun to sit with the lads. We told jokes and played games much in the fashion of family gatherings at home. Hum did his high-altitude nose trick – the idea was that someone rubbed their scent on an item, such as an empty bottle, and Hum, who had not been present in the room, would make his entrance and after some theatricals would point to the item. He got it right every time. Excellent fun, we later learnt how, but that was his secret, so no disclosures here.

Another early start to the day, but a leisurely one. However, it was a steep start once walking. I was told to take short slow steps which would help with the breathlessness. It did. Thank you, Ashish. I was also glad of my walking poles which greatly helped my balance, very important in some areas. Nicky and Paul and their porters walked on ahead, chatting and stopping for the perfect photographic opportunities.

We traversed up the Dzong Khola valley to Ranipauwa. We were now at 3,000 + metres above sea level – OMG. We stopped at a small hotel called the Bob Marley, no prizes for guessing what the theme was there. Jamaican colours, and many pictures of the man, provided by the many trekkers who had passed that way.

Finally, we reached our goal, standing at 3,7100 metres (12,172 feet above sea level) – Muktinath, located at the bottom of the Thorong La pass. Known in the Hindu religion as Mukti Kshetra, 'the place of salvation', or in Buddhist terms as Chumig Gyatsa, 'the place of 100 waters'.

A sacred place of pilgrimage for both religions, where people were known to have walked to from as far away as India.

There were two Shrines, one was the Vishnu Mandir with its 108 water spouts shaped as cow's heads, where the faithful would anoint their heads in the water.

Many coloured prayer flags fluttered in the wind symbolising different elements and energies. Both Hindu and Buddhist religions were represented.

The Prayer flags were brightly coloured and each with a particular meaning – Red for fire and heat energy, Green for water, nature and motion, Yellow for earth, Blue for sky, purity and healing and White for wind. They had written mantras on them and the names of four powerful animals (dragon, garuda, snow lion and tiger). In the centre there sits a depiction of a horse called Lungta, which in Tibetan means Wind Horse. They are used to promote wisdom, peace, compassion and strength, their message being carried to all on the breeze.

We also visited the other shrine, Mebar Lha Gomba, which enclosed the eternal blue flame of natural gas, which burnt forever above a tiny fountain of water.

A coming together of fire, water and air, a place of homage for all.

Nicky and I were given the Hindu Tika blessing, which involved the painting of the yellow and red stain on our foreheads. I asked for prayers to be said for two friends who were, at the time, undergoing chemotherapy.

A tranquil place, the silence only broken by us, although we were very respectful. I felt really at peace there, as did we all. I took a number of photographs and then it was time for the 'cake ritual'.

These were the two cakes that I had been given by Joan on leaving for Nepal. I shared them out between the ten of us and explained how she had always wanted to visit this sacred place but was now too old and infirm.

The cakes were very rich fruit cakes, which I think the lads were a little apprehensive of at first, but, I think to please me, they did eat. The crumbs that were left in the tins were scattered around the ground, so that something that had been touched by Joan also touched that holy place.

We walked back down the hill, so much more quickly than on the way up. My breathing had been really laboured, but once I slowed my pace it improved. Amazingly, at no point did my legs ache.

On our return journey to Jharkot, we noticed that there had been a slight snowfall on the hills but thought no more about it as our evening meal was our main priority.

We had a wonderful evening, talking, laughing, playing magic tricks. I even managed to win some money by pulling a 100 rupee note from between one upright and one upturned coke bottle. My first attempt saw the top bottle clatter to the table, but on my second, to everyone's amazement (mostly mine), I pulled the note cleanly leaving the two bottles standing. Apparently, I was the first of any trekking party they had been with, to do it – or so they told me.

It was a cold night, and we awoke to find everywhere covered in a thick carpet of snow.

Chapter Six

The road to Marpha

We had our breakfast and looked out to see that the snow was still falling. An animated discussion between Bridget, Barry and the porters took place as to whether we could continue on. It had been known for people to be snowed in for months on the higher passes.

I thought about home and my job if that were to be the outcome. There was no point in worrying, as that would have been futile. We were at the mercy of Mother Nature, and it was not as if a vehicle could come to rescue us. In fact, we had not seen any vehicles since we had flown into Jomsom. Animal trains and footwork were the forms of transport here.

Finally, the snow stopped after a couple of hours, the sun broke through the clouds and the journey was on. There were some stirrings in the village as women appeared on the flat rooftops, sweeping away the snow.

More activity on a grander scale as trekkers and porters appeared from all corners. The sounds of impatient animals were heard from the houses. Some of the porters were poorly equipped for the conditions, no heavy-duty clothing and only flip-flops on their feet. I felt sorry for them. Our porters, however, were provided with all such cold weather wear, as were we.

The scenery, spectacular at any time, was truly dazzling. A layer of snow, about six inches, lay over everything and crunched under our feet as we began to make our way back down to the valley. I really began to feel like an intrepid traveller, or climber, even though there was no mountaineering involved. These were the kinds of views that they must have had when pitting themselves against the mountains.

Still, I had to say this was enough snow for me, I had never been a winter sports type of a person, although spontaneous snowball fights broke out – I guess you never quite grow up.

Ashish walked with me and provided a steadying hand all the way down, although for whose sake that was I was not quite sure.

He was from southern Nepal where snow was a rarity. I took lots of photographs and thought how different everywhere looked from just a few days ago.

The sun, once it had taken a proper hold on the day, became very hot, so it became a case of shedding layers until I got to my T-shirt. The physical exertions of the walking also added to the temperature.

The vista changed as we got lower down, and we spent our time clambering over rocks and fording the now fuller streams. We walked for about eight hours, punctuated by short stops, mainly to drink some fluids, but not really staying anywhere very long.

My legs had begun to ache, using different muscle groups I suppose, on the downward journey.

Every time there was the slightest obstacle, out of nowhere, hands would appear to help you over or under it. These lads were really quite something. They referred to me as 'older sister', a term of endearment in reference to my age, me being a good 20 years older than Nicky and Paul.

Sante collected some stones, which he presented to me. He must have heard me express a wish to take some small ones home. The gorge in the distant past had been a part of the Tethys Sea, thrown up to these heights during the collision of the land masses and the formation of the Himalayas. Ammonites could be found.

They were all so intuitive, you just knew that if your life was in jeopardy they would do their utmost to save you. Sante very much reminded me of the soldiers I had met in Brunei; strong, silent but not unfriendly, and not above a good giggle like the other lads.

Finally, we reached Marpha, having crossed the Kali Gandaki River at the suspension bridge at Piling. I had fun on the bridge, bouncing up and down like a happy schoolgirl, much to the consternation of the others on the bridge. They were not impressed. Ah well, I need to learn that although I do not have a height phobia that does not apply to everyone.

Marpha was a thriving little town and we were taken to the Paradise Guest House, our rest stop for the night. It suited its name, there was electricity, an attached bathroom, hot water, carpets and a proper sit-down toilet – wow.

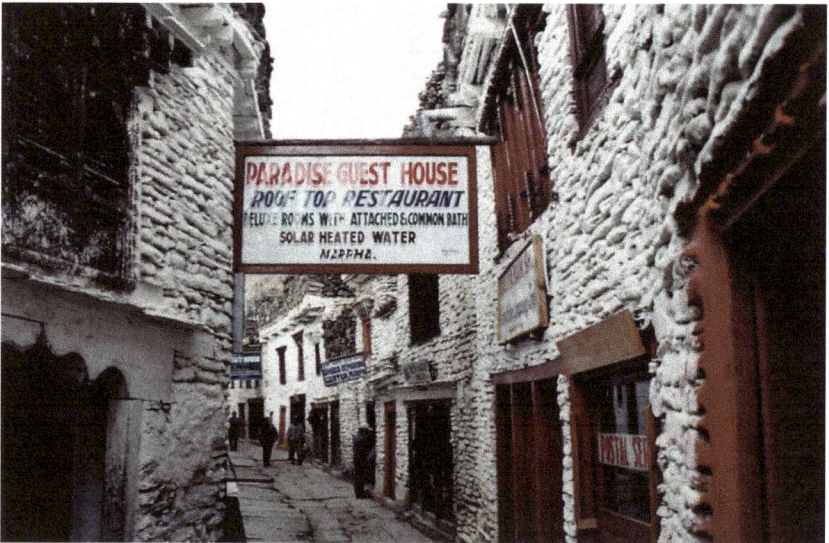

Toilets vary greatly in Nepal, depending on where you are. It is not necessarily to do with being on a trail, because even ones in lodges and hotels could be a cubicle with ceramic footprints over a squatting area. Outside, it was a matter of finding the place of most privacy. No wonder the ladies wear long dresses, saris etc.

Having been in the TA, and on holidays with basic facilities, I did not find it too difficult. Needs must.

Our porters had been carrying our large rucksacks for all of our walking time, so it must have been a relief to off-load them for a while. I had a bath, what bliss, changed and went with Bridget for a wander around the town. Nicky, Paul, Barry and some of the lads had gone to play pool. We joined them in a small, dim, seedy pool hall, where the sound of the balls being struck was accompanied by music from U2 and Bob Marley. In the gloom, we could see pictures of Bob on the walls. We could have been anywhere on the planet, it was great.

Dorjee spent the whole time giggling, in fact they all giggled, they had a sort of innocence about them that was very refreshing. We spent the evening in the guest house bar until bed time (which was 8pm – early nights and very early morning starts). I got talking to a Japanese lad, Kiyoshi, who had been just about everywhere, including Tibet, and an older German guy, Gerhardt. We three sat, exchanged stories and put the world to rights, our versions anyway.

Chapter Seven

Dhaulagiri and Kalopani

8.00am, a really late start compared to other mornings. It was a lovely day, but cold, the puddles we saw on the way were still frozen. Out came the cold weather coats.

Again, the trail took us along the Kali Gandaki gorge. We could have been on the moon walking in this strange landscape.

We saw many mule trains carrying their wares, their cowbells tinkling on the air, warning of their coming. We were reminded that it was our responsibility to get out of their way.

It was a day of long stretches of walking, although we did have our tea breaks. The lads could be heard singing as they followed the trail. The views as expected were fantastic, and then in the distance we saw Dhaulagiri.

I shall do my best to describe to you the magnificence of this mountain, but any words used fall short of the reality of the sight that was in front of our eyes.

It stood before us in all of its glory, with wisps of white clouds that swirled around its summit, and the glacier that tumbled down the slopes which glistened in the sunlight. It absolutely stopped us in our tracks, we were 15 miles away and it still dominated the scene. To say we were in awe nowhere near describes the feeling. I had never in my lifetime experienced such majesty, I was dumbstruck.

It was fanciful, I know, but I thought of that mountain as female, with her dazzling skirts that fell around her, much in the way that I thought of Everest as having male traits, flexing his muscles as he pointed skywards.

Sadly, we had to move on to our next overnight stop.

The scenery had started to change from a treeless, rock-strewn landscape to that of a more forested region. There were more villages at this lower altitude and, of course, walking downhill was far less taxing on the breathing. We followed the edge of the canyon along the rock paths, saw some cliff caves and also a vehicle, a tractor. Interesting. We wondered how that got up there.

We saw a group of traders, from the Mustang area.

We eventually came to the small town of Kalopani (Black Water) where there were magnificent views of Annapurna I. The evening was approaching, and we saw a herd of sheep and goats being driven towards the safety of the town confines. Some isolated houses lined the route to the concentration of buildings that constituted the small town. We passed under the town gate, through the cobbled streets to our lodge.

Our resting place for the night was a solid looking lodge with eating quarters at the front, then over a courtyard to the sleeping area. The rooms in many of the lodges were partitioned off from each other with hardboard sheets. Visual separation from other people, but not aural. Not that it mattered, that was part of the fun of it all.

Somewhere in the building was a man and his young son. He had the deepest voice I have ever heard, complete with a Texan drawl straight out of the movies. When we saw him at breakfast, well no wonder, he looked as if he was seven feet tall with snow-white hair; an imposing guy who, to me, was the personification of the mountains outside.

But back to the evening, before our meal we went up on the roof terrace and watched the sun setting over the mountains. Pure gold, what a sight. Sadly, the image did not stay for long, darkness fell, and with the sun gone the temperature plummeted.

The lodge had 'hot tables', square communal tables surrounded by benches, underneath which were heating boxes, a little like Victorian warming pans.

The warmth was particularly welcome on cold nights. Back inside, we continued talking into the night and exchanged stories about our day. My walking pace was slower than the others, so the evenings were our catch-up time.

There was always so much to see, the smiling people who greeted us as we walked through their villages, daily life going on all around, the sights, the smells of cooking, the children on their way to school.

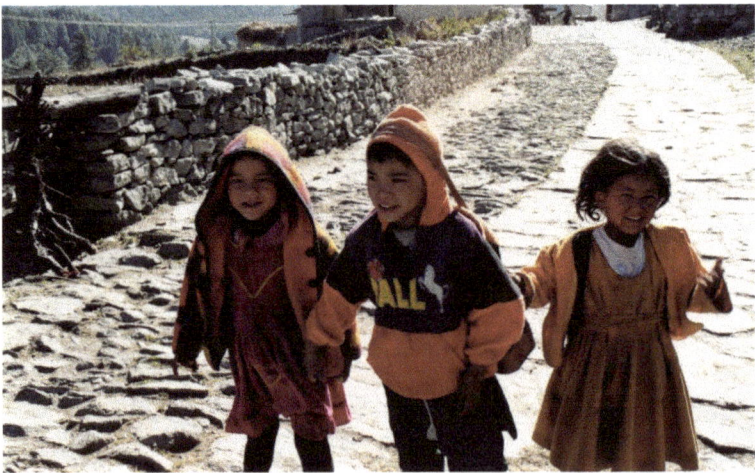

Most importantly to me was the feeling of being part of a group, seeing the most spectacular sights on earth. I took many photographs in the hope that they would reflect some of the splendour.

Not such an early rise, we moved off at about 09.30am, really late in trekking terms. The air had warmed up by then, one thing about walking in the early mornings, the air was cold and made our noses run, thus a plentiful supply of tissues was required.

Some of the trails were quite precarious, but as always there was a helping hand there when needed. We were walking downhill now, a drop of 700m. The terrain constantly changed and became more forested. We arrived at a lodge where we had the most delicious tomato soup made from the tomatoes that grew by the door. Many of the items on the menus were grown at the lodges. I had a shower and spent time in the room writing up my diary.

Nicky and Paul really hit it off, it was nice to see. I did my own thing, which in the main was eating, sleeping and taking photographs. That was why our catch ups were so good.

We went for a stroll around the town, saw a lovely waterfall, well worth the difficulty in getting to it. Later, in our room, Nicky and I got the giggles and we could not stop. Our laughter took on a life of its own. Each time we got it under control, we would hear the lads in a downstairs room laughing, at us we were sure, and of course it started us off again. Noisy night.

We really needed to sleep, we had a seven hour walk ahead of us.

Chapter Eight

Tatopani and Shikha

I had an unsettled night, but surprisingly woke up pretty refreshed. There was a knock on our door. Outside was Hum making sure we were ready to go. We said yes, give us five minutes, and shut the door. There was a knock immediately. What! On opening the door, we were met with the sight of the whole party standing, looking at their watches, no words just looking. Ha, Ha.

The sun shone as we set off on the next section of our adventure.

It was not as bad as I had thought it would be, downhill for a start. Again, the scenery was beautiful. It felt like summer, the cherry trees were in bloom, vegetable fields displaying their bounty, a waterfall tumbling down the odd cliff face. We saw young children walking the paths, going off to schools that could be hours of walking away. Such hardy people, whose training obviously started at a very early age.

We stopped a number of times for a drink and an energy bar, even though it was a long walk it was not too demanding. My fitness levels must have improved because I managed the meandering trail quite well. We crossed more suspension bridges, I just loved them, stepped aside for a mule train to pass.

We then carried on to our next stop.

That was to be Ghasa. We had passed some smallholdings built into the cliff face, and an area where there had been a landslide. The army had been called to dynamite away the rocks that had fallen into the river, causing a blockage which could have led to flooding upstream. We saw women and older children at work in the fields, and later we stopped to watch an elderly lady grinding corn between two large stones, something she had done for decades.

We walked through a very picturesque village called Dana, where we saw all aspects of life going on; household chores, corn sheaths hanging from the house rafters, wood being gathered and stored, and men and beasts tilling the fields, and women bringing in the harvest. Life, as it had gone on for centuries.

In contrast, we saw many trekkers drinking beer at the roadside bars.

The sun shone brightly and the whole scene was framed by the mountains. What more could we need or want? Of course, we were not unaware that we were just travelling through, but for those who lived there it was very different, this was one of the poorest nations on earth.

Later in the evening we watched the glorious sunset over Annapurna I and Khangshar Kang.

61

The next day we went on to Tatopani, a thriving little bazaar town, the name means 'hot springs', which were situated near the river's edge. We were booked into the Dhaulagiri Lodge, one of the prettiest we had seen so far.

The gardens with their rows of vibrantly coloured flowers sparkled in the sunlight, added to which there was a large vegetable patch with produce of every kind. The room, too, was befitting of the beauty of the place with everything laid on for our comfort.

I decided to go down to the hot springs, so donned my bathing suit and caftan, and with my towel, ventured forth.

You must always be mindful of the culture and not walk about half dressed. The pool was really good, like a hot bath at home. It certainly made my aching legs feel a lot better. There were a number of people in the pool of different nationalities. We all, after silent acknowledgement of each other, sat back, relaxed and let the water do its magic.

It was going to be Nicky's birthday in a couple of days, so later Paul and I managed to sneak off to buy some presents. I really enjoyed that little town, a friendly happy place.

After our meal we sat out on the roof terrace, chatted and watched as the townspeople and their animals returned home at sunset.

No vehicles, no sirens, no loud TVs, just occasional soft voices, the odd baa from the sheep and the deep sighs of the yaks. And, of course, the stars were out in abundance – could you ever ask for better?

I slept well and joined the others at breakfast for a team talk. We all opted for a change in our itinerary which involved a trek to Shikha, another climb of 2000 feet. At that juncture it was not so daunting, as we had all become acclimatised and were much fitter in mind and body. We were told that the scenery was worth the climb, and it was.

Much more rural, we passed many farms. Also, a myriad of crop terraces that defined the countryside, spread out like a quilt of many colours. We even saw some water buffalo, massive beasts, lumbering through the countryside.

Everywhere the people were so friendly, it did not matter to whom you spoke, just saying "Namaste" made everyone smile. What was not a smiling matter was seeing the tattered Maoist flags hanging from the trees.

What little TV we did see at the lodges reported on the extent of the incursions and sadly the daily death count.

The mountains were behind us and we felt that we were being guarded by huge white-haired giants keeping us safe. As we walked on, the sun started to go down and suddenly the tracks were filled with people and animals returning home. Their equivalent of rush hour, I supposed.

As each lodge provided the same menu, we were able to order our meals in advance. Ashish saw to that each day. Our porters were wonderful lads, all very different in personality and looks. As they were from different areas of Nepal, their features reflected that. Ashish, Amrit and Dorjee I guess were in their twenties, Hum in his thirties and Sante was in his early forties. You felt that you could entrust your life to them, especially Sante who reminded me of the Gurkha soldiers I had met in Brunei.

Home for the night, and following our meal, it was time for some entertainment. Barry and the lads entertained us with Nepali folk songs and dances. It was interesting to see the subtle differences in styles from the different regions. They informed us that the next night was going to be our turn to perform. Panic. What could we sing that would represent England? Still, that was for tomorrow, tonight was their turn and very good it was too, such talented people.

Chapter Nine

Ghorepani and Happy Birthdays

It was Nicky's birthday, so I sang, or rather croaked my way through a version of the famous ditty.

We had a good breakfast, then got our drinks ready. This consisted, as it had done on every other morning, of filling our flasks with boiled water. The taste was, well, disgusting, even with the flavoured glucose tablets, but the need for it absolutely overrode everything else. We tried not to use bottled water, as the disposal of the plastic bottles was a real problem, especially as many people just discarded them at the roadside.

The trail was all uphill and had not yet dried up from the early morning mist. From our vantage point, we saw a school with the children lined up ready to go inside to their classes.

A universal scene which could have been a school yard in any part of the world. We also saw people carrying supplies, for food and for home-building.

No white delivery vans here. I was impressed, I was having enough trouble just carrying my daypack, but they, like our porters, strolled ahead scarcely out of breath.

As tiredness started to seep in, the small town of Ghorepani came into sight. A mixture of local houses, and lodges with their blue roofs, the main street filled with small shops and stalls run by Tibetan traders.

There were many steps up, but as always, the views compensated. Some of the paths had reminded me of Storeton Woods on the Wirral after the rain. The smell of damp wood on the air evoked some lovely memories.

After lunch, we went sightseeing in the forest, through rhododendron trees, climbed over stumps and tree roots covered with lichen and listened to the bird songs. Then later, we, like the other animals, returned home for the evening. As with other towns and villages in the region, the whole view was framed by the magnificent mountains. Our plan for the next day was to ascend Poon Hill to watch the sunrise.

We stayed in a large lodge with many other trekking parties. A lovely, noisy place, with chatter in many languages. After our meal, we had a lovely surprise, the kitchen staff had made Nicky a birthday cake.

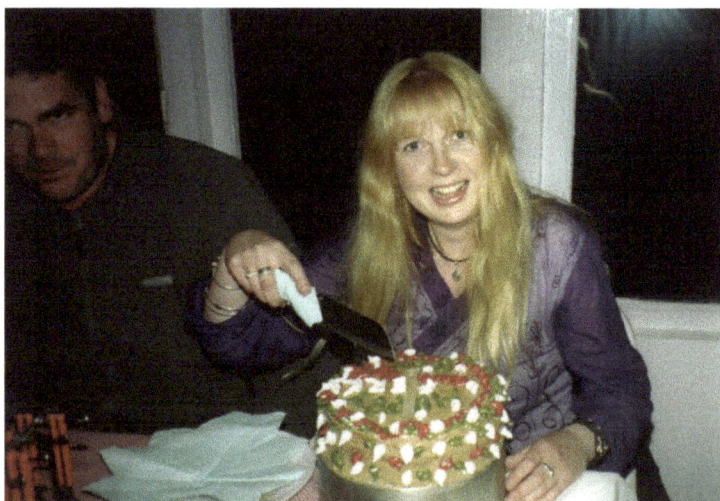

She was delighted. Apparently, it had all been arranged when Sante went ahead to book the accommodation. We had started to sing the birthday song when the whole lodge joined in. We gave her our presents; the lads had bought things too. It was a lovely moment, what a memory. There were, as you can imagine, a few tears.

We went happily to bed. We had a very early wake-up call for the trip up Poon Hill but, unfortunately, the early morning mist obliterated everything, so the trip was called off. Back to bed.

Another early start, we had a really long day ahead of us. We had to reach the Pokhara road to meet up with our jeep, which would take us back to civilisation. A seven hour walk at least.

We started off through a forest region, as always, the scenery was stunning. From the hillsides, we saw more crop terraces, animals out in the fields, and children on their way to school. We stopped for a tea break at the top of the ridge. Our next stop would be lunch at Tikhun, but first there were the steps at Ullery to deal with, we had been warned that there were a few steps there on the downward hill. We went down about 20 steps, then it flattened out.

'That wasn't so bad' I thought, 'what was all the fuss about?', but of course, that was just the taster, as I realised when the other 3,900 came into view. OMG, I felt every one of them. As well as the number of them, they were of different heights and widths.

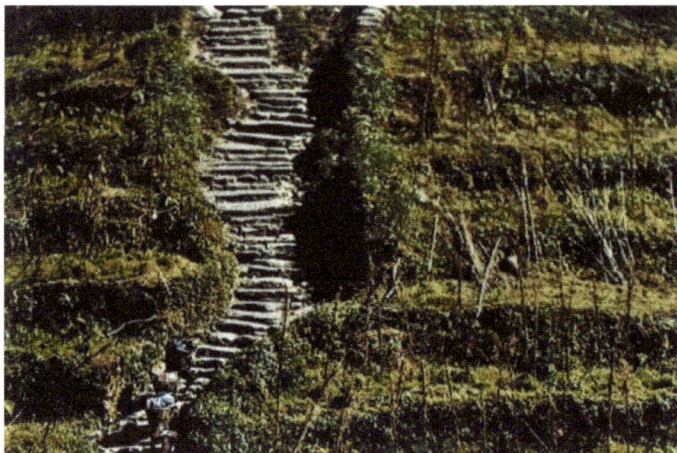

It got to the point where my legs would not support me, lactic acid build-up was affecting my muscles. My travelling companion was Amrit, who patiently sat with me and massaged my legs. After a short while, Sante appeared to see what had happened. He spoke at length with Amrit. I, meanwhile, had a serious talk with myself, albeit silently, about the situation. I reckoned that the only thing that would get me off that hill, was a helicopter, and that was very unlikely as I wasn't actually injured. The rest and the massage began to work, and I got unsteadily to my feet and continued down the hill. Once Sante saw I was up and walking he went off, leaving me with my faithful and extremely helpful guide Amrit. My unsteadiness improved with each step.

As we walked, I realised that Sante had come back minus his large rucksack, and I knew then that he had come to carry me.

We finally reached our lunch stop only 25 minutes after the others had arrived. I was met with a round of applause, for determination I guess, but really the plaudit should have been for Amrit. Once again, I had been very impressed by the help and respect given to me by all of our guides, and in fact, the whole party.

The muscles in my legs were still screaming, and we still had a full four hours of walking ahead of us before we reached the

Pokhara road. However, after a while, I was so absorbed in what was around me I stopped noticing the pain.

At one point the clouds parted, and we were treated to a view of Machhapuchhre, just visible in the distance.

The magnificence of the scenery never ceased to amaze me. It was a cure for all ills, even aching legs.

We walked on through woodland, over small streams with their rickety bridges, and other flag-festooned suspension bridges over the wider rivers.

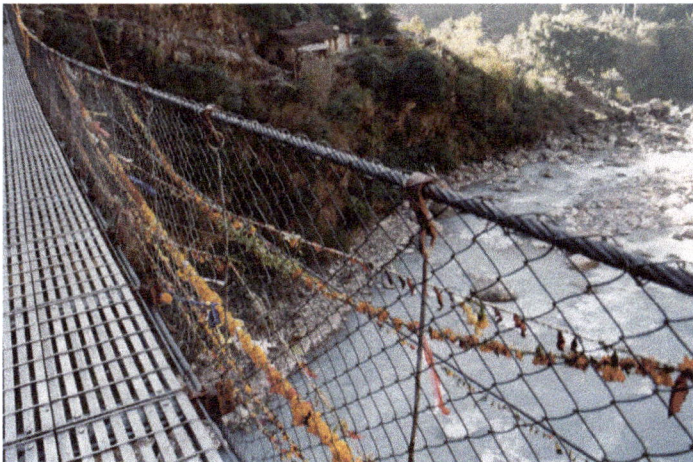

The last one we crossed was a rope type with a slatted wooden walkway. As soon as I was on it, the lads jumped on the other end and proceeded to bounce me all the way across. Payment in full for what I had done to them on the other bridges. We all laughed and laughed.

As we neared the road, we started to see more villages, terraces and people working the fields.

As we reached Birethanti, on the border of the Conservation Area, traits of 'civilisation' were there in abundance.

It looked dirty, ramshackle, with broken down vehicles and people with a poorness about them. Such a change from the villages we had seen on the trail.

We reached the Pokhara road and rested while we waited for the transport. I realised that this was the finish of the trekking part of the adventure and felt sad that it had come to an end. Suddenly I felt an overwhelming tiredness and slept the whole way back to Pokhara.

Chapter Ten

Pokhara, Kathmandu and Home

We had booked back into the hotel where we had originally stayed and had luckily left some of our baggage so that the lads would have less to carry. We had been shocked at the heavily laden porters we had seen at Jomsom.

Before going to our rooms, we posed for a group photograph, all present except for Bridget.

It was good to be back in a hotel room, although being in the wilds certainly had its compensations with the company and the scenery. Next morning, after a very leisurely breakfast we went shopping, mainly for goods to be brought home as presents. There was plenty of choice, Pokhara was such a lively vibrant place with people, shops, animals, vehicles, noise and bustle everywhere.

After lunch and a rest, we went shopping again. Nicky and Paul wandered off, I went back to the lakeside to see the Tibetan lady from whom I had bought my bracelet. I received a warm welcome as she recognized me and asked me to recount my experiences.

On the way back, I passed the Summer Palace complex. The guard outside, a young soldier, looked my way, so I said Namaste. He responded and his face broke into the biggest smile. He brought his rifle up into the traditional hands together pose for the greeting. A lovely moment.

Later we had a really good meal at a Tibetan restaurant. It was called a 'Steamboat Meal', a mixture of meat and vegetables in a clear spiced soup, served straight from the cooking pot in the middle of the table. Delicious. It was just five of us, Bridget, Barry, Nicky, Paul and me; the lads had gone on ahead to Kathmandu (KM) to make the final arrangements.

On leaving, the staff at the hotel gave us parting gifts, prayer scarves and beautifully embossed envelopes and paper. It was all very emotional.

The flight was very good, very little turbulence and the views, as always, spectacular. We could see the Annapurna range poking out of the clouds, and in the clear patches we could see down to the forests and terraces. Beautiful.

We arrived at Kathmandu and went to our hotel, our original 'home'. Out for lunch and got a little lost as we tried to find the 'Third Eye' restaurant. Ironic, I thought, but we managed to see a lot of KM life.

Back to the hotel for a bath, oh luxury, and made ready for our last evening meal. We had a laugh with Bridget and Barry, we had had the most amazing time with them on the trek and I am sure that we benefited from their well of knowledge. As we were a much smaller party, I, for one, felt more engaged with everything.

A new day and it was time to move on, this time back to the UK and home. I felt quite sad, strangely mixed up emotions.

Hum and Dorjee arrived to help with the baggage. There was something happening, there was a large police presence on the streets and a great feeling of unrest. They were not able to get the van into the Thamel district, so they came to help carry everything. Ashish stayed with the van. Sadly, we did not get to see Amrit and Sante to say farewell, but our last images were of three smiling faces waving goodbye.

Goodbye also to Bridget and Barry. Now we were at the airport again, it did not seem nearly a month since we had arrived, and here we were going home. But oh, what memories we were taking with us. Checking in presented no problems, then on to the plane. Somewhat larger than what we had travelled on in the past weeks. We were to stage at Abu Dhabi and Bahrain. However, the holiday mood was still very evident on the first leg of the journey, with singing and dancing in the aisles.

We touched down at Heathrow. What a shock, it was wet and cold. We had forgotten it was December in England, we had been sunshine spoilt for the past month. I had a slight panic about all of my films as they went through the X-ray machines for a second time.

Sandra and her niece and nephew were waiting for us when we finally arrived back in Birkenhead. Hugs all around. I got home, kettle on, said hello to my cats. Then sleep. I had loved the travelling but now I was happy to be home, my Zen place. I could not wait to have my photographs developed so I could relive my experiences, and what absolutely stunning, amazing, beautiful, spectacular experiences they were too.

(Thank you to all concerned, especially the 'lads' for all of their hard work)

"NAMASTE"

Postscript

Some reminiscences of what I saw, when "I simply looked…"
Majestic mountains, by day and night.
Star laden skies.
Small villages hugging the hillsides.
Porters.
Rivers and river beds.
Deep gorges.
Huge boulders.
Green forests.
Eagles, kingfishers, redstarts.
Monkeys.
Children with runny noses (altitude affliction).
People of different cultures.
Timber mills.
Wheel of Life.
Corn threshing.
Yak, cow, and mule trains.
Goats, sheep and water buffalo.
Old dogs that followed for miles.
Huge satellite discs.
Traditional folk music.
Singing and dancing.
Waterfalls.
Suspension bridges.
Maoist flags.
Hot springs.
Tropical gardens.
Prayer flags blowing in the breeze.
Snow.
School children.
Landslides.
Bridget, Barry, Hum, Ashish, Amrit, Dorjee, Sante, Nicky and Paul.

Appendix

Transport

Coach	National Express	
	Birkenhead – London – Birkenhead	

Tube	London Underground (various)

Air	Gulf Air	London – Abu Dhabi – Kathmandu
	Gulf Air	Kathmandu – Abu Dhabi – London
	Buddha Air	Everest Sightseeing Trip
	Nepal Air	Pokhara to Jomsom
	Nepal Air	Pokhara to Kathmandu

Road	Jeep	Kathmandu to Pokhara
	Jeep	Birethanti to Pokhara

On Foot	Jomsom, Eklebhatti, Kagbeni, Muktinath, Marpha, Kalopani, Tatopani, Shikha, Ghasa, Dana, Ghorepani, Poon Hill, Birethanti

Permissions
Nepal Visa
Entry Visa / Fee for the Annapurna Conservation Area

Medical
Inoculations: An international Inoculation Passport, with listed Blood Group. Advisable to get combined Tetanus / Diphtheria, Hepatitis A and B, Meningitis cover.

Kit and Equipment List (suggestions)
Comfortable walking boots
Walking sandals
Anorak

Fleece
T-shirts
Trousers and over trousers (rain)
Socks
Thermal underwear
Hat
Gloves
Sleeping Bag
Roll up mattress
Walking poles
Sunglasses
Large Rucksack
Day Pack
Travel Towel
Toilet gear
Medical Pack
Water Bottle
Eating utensils
Whistle and compass
Note book and pen
Camera
Waterproof bag for paperwork etc.
Some form of lock
Any other kit as recommended by your trekking company.

Lodges and Hotels

Kantipur Temple House	Kathmandu
Hotel Stupa	Pokhara
Hotel Mona Lisa	Jomsom
Annapurna Lodge	Kagbeni
New Plaza	Jharkot
Paradise Hotel	Marpha
Hotel Bob Marley (visit)	Marpha
Lodge	Kalopani
Eagles Nest Lodge	Ghasa
Dhaulagiri Lodge	Tatopani
Shanti Lodge	Shikha
Sunny Lodge	Ghorepani

Miscellaneous
3900 + steps at Ullery
Various Tea Houses
Various Temples and Monasteries
Photocopies of important paperwork, passport, visas, permits etc.

Glossary
Annapurna – Goddess of abundance
Bhatti – Tea House
Chiya – sweet tea with milk and spices
Chomolungma – Goddess Mother of the World
Chumig Gyatsa – Hundred Waters
Dalai Lama – High Priest of Tibetan Buddhism
Doko – basket using a head strap
Ganesh – elephant-headed son of Shiva and Parvati
Ghat – riverside platform for cremations
Harmika – eyes on a stupa to face all four directions
Himal – range or snowy peak
Kumari – young virgin regarded as a living goddess in Kathmandu
        valley towns.
Lungta – Wind Horse
Mandala – sacred diagram in Buddhism
Mani stones – rocks inscribed with Tibetan prayers in high areas
Mebar Lha Gomba – Miraculous Fire
Mukti Kshetra – Place of Salvation
Namaste – "I salute the divinity within you"
Pahil nai eka cha – "Already got one."
Parvati – Shiva's consort
Sagarmatha – Forehead in the sky, Peak of Heaven, Everest
Shiva – chief Hindu God
Stupa – Buddhist, bell shaped temple
Tika – a powder mark applied on the forehead, between the eyes,
        a symbol of the presence of the divine.
Yaks – Nepalese cattle

Index

www.ingramcontent.com/pod-product-compliance
Lightning Source LLC
LaVergne TN
LVHW010309070426
835511LV00021B/3454